Denisovans

The Archaic Humans of the

Paleolithic Period

Table of Contents

Introduction 1

Chapter One: Background 5

Denisova Cave 6

Geographic and Climate Conditions Around
Denisova 10

The Field of Paleoanthropology 13

Chapter Two: The Human Family 17

Human Evolution 17

Neanderthals 21

Other Species and Early Modern Humans 23

Early Modern Humans and Neanderthals 26

Chapter Three: The Discoveries at Denisova 29

Initial Discoveries and the Beginning of
Research... 30

Further Findings.. 33

Other Prehistoric Discoveries at Denisova 36

Chapter Four: Denny 41

Research and Identification................................. 44

Other Revelations... 49

Chapter Five: Other Denisovan
            Characteristics and Evidence 53
    Appearance and Additional Findings.............. 53
    The Xiahe Mandible 55
    Baishiya Karst Cave 61

Chapter Six: An Archaic People 65
    Demographics.. 66
    The Appearance Discussion 69
    The Future of Denisovan Study 72

Chapter Seven: The Genetic Legacy of
            Our Cousins.....................................76
    A History of Intermingling 77
    The Results 80
    Red Deer Cave People... 84

Conclusion...88

References 90

Introduction

Even with all our modern technology and advanced science, we still know relatively little about the origins of our fascinating species. We have an idea about the natural processes that have led to the emergence of Homo sapiens as we know ourselves today as well as the nature of some of our ancestors. We also possess insight into other archaic human species that we once shared this planet with. Even though we have these bits of information and a general picture of what happened, much about our origins and early history remains mysterious.

This isn't as much the result of technological and scientific shortcomings as it is a consequence of a scarcity of evidence—the more anthropology ventures beyond Africa, the less evidence it encounters. Still, thanks to our advanced technology and scientific methods, each shred of evidence is incredibly valuable and can tell us many stories about times long gone. The value of even the smallest bits of fossil evidence, for example, has been well-illustrated by the relatively recent discoveries in a particular cave in southern Russia. By extracting DNA samples from tiny bone fragments, scientists have identified what some now believe is a new human species that once coexisted with us and has even managed to pass on a bit of their DNA to us.

Depending on who is asked, the species or sub-species are the increasingly famous Denisovans, named after the cave where their remains were first identified. These long-gone folks were initially mistaken for Neanderthals, so the latter findings came as quite a shock to paleoanthropologists. The controversy surrounding the taxonomy debate has revolved only around how we should classify these Denisovans, which in no way diminishes the important differences that have been identified between these archaic people and us.

So far, DNA has been the leading source of information and has given us virtually all the answers that we have. Even so, this evidence has and continues to be a goldmine of valuable insights into who these people were. Until these discoveries, paleoanthropologists believed that early Homo sapiens and Neanderthals were the only archaic human species that coexisted as our close historical cousins. The discovery of Denisovans has challenged these views thoroughly and has also ignited the imagination of many researchers, sparking legitimate questions about just how many cousin species we might have had.

In expectation of new discoveries that could bring more answers, we have plenty of questions and evidence to evaluate regarding what we have found thus far, which will keep researchers occupied for years to come. This book will help you get acquainted with what anthropologists and archeologists have found and who these mysterious cousins might have been. You should also walk away with a better understanding of human origins, prehistory, and how our ancestors lived and coexisted with similar yet very different archaic humans. Denisovans are proving to be a very important piece of this great puzzle, and learning about them might prove to be of utmost importance to understanding how and where we came from.

Chapter One:

Background

The Denisova Cave is the only locale from which evidence about Denisovans has been extracted. According to this evidence, these people may have shown up at this particular locale as early as 200-300,000 years ago. At the same time, it has also been confirmed that they were around 55,000 ago, which was comparatively recent. This means that the Denisovans inhabited the Altai Mountains for a very long time before going extinct. The exact extent of their range is something that's still being determined, although we already know they have reached far and wide.

The scarcity of evidence or, more accurately, the low number of sources of evidence that we have has thus far been the most limiting factor in Denisovan research. It's certainly possible that Denisovan remains will be identified in a new location at some point, but it's very difficult to say where that might be yet.

Some of the most important discoveries regarding Denisovans have been very recent, going back just a couple of years, as you will learn through this book. To start with, however, we will take a look at some background information and context that will help introduce you to the new and exciting field of study that Denisovans have spawned.

Denisova Cave

The Denisova Cave has been a true treasure trove for paleoanthropologists, with numerous invaluable finds that have given insight into 40,000 years of history. The discoveries in this Siberian cave have given us a lot of information about humans and animals, such as horses, for instance.

To be exact, the Denisova Cave is located in the Soloneshensky District of the Altai Krai administrative region and federal unit of Russia. The location of the cave is not far from the point where Russia, China, Mongolia, and Kazakhstan converge. In the Bashelaksky Range of the Altai Mountains, this cave is situated in a rough, mountainous locale that has been continuously inhabited for at least 50,000 years. Who it was exactly that inhabited this region has been the subject of a lot of interest and research for quite a while now, with an emphasis on a Neanderthal presence, among others.

The Denisova Cave is a limestone cave comprising 270 square meters or 2,900 square feet, divided into three main parts, including the main, south, and east chambers. The main chamber's open floor is around 30 x 36 feet (9 x 11 m), providing a decent living space. The fossil remains that researchers have been extracting for decades now are found in the cave sediments, which are rich in remains of people but also all sorts of animals. This suggests that the cave has been around for a long time and a very popular place providing natural shelter. Many species of animals have been identified from these remains, including extinct ones.

The closest settlement is a small village by the name of Chorny Anui, while the administrative center of the Altai region, Barnaul, is around 93 miles (150 km) to the north. The cave is located at an elevation of 2,297 ft (700 m) above sea level and is not far up from the Anuy River, a tributary of the Ob.

The name of the cave dates back to the 18th century when a Russian hermit by the name of Dyonisiy, the Russian version of Denis, lived in it. This man was an Old Believer, a practitioner of an old-time form of Russian Orthodox Christianity. However, among the indigenous Altai locals, the cave was and still is called the Bear Rock (Ayu-Tash).

We will go into more detail on the early discoveries and research in the Denisova Cave, but scientific endeavors generally began in the 1970s when the first archeological and fossil evidence was found. The identification and major research relating to Denisovans, however, began much more recently. There are 22 layers of sediment in the Denisova Cave, as far as we know for certain, and they date back to a period between the life of Denis and prehistoric times some 125-180,000 years ago.

The cave itself provides some rather good conditions for DNA preservation in fossils. According to Tom Higham of the Radiocarbon Accelerator Unit at Oxford University, the cave is perfectly cool and thus ensures that there isn't much disintegration of the DNA samples still contained in the bones. The problem, however, is that the bones have been frequently found and chewed on by various animals, especially hyenas and similar beasts of opportunity. This is why so many of the Denisova Cave bones are little more than ground-down fragments that litter the floor and the sediment layers beneath. When a new fragment is found, it's usually impossible to visually identify what creature it even comes from, which is why DNA research has been so important for the research at this site. Despite all that, Tom Higham and many other scientists consider the Denisova Cave a true treasure trove.

The problem with genetic research is that DNA extraction and sequencing are long, painstaking processes. This is barely a factor when working with several samples, but the thousands of bone fragments and other fossil evidence from the Denisova Cave require quite a bit of effort. This is probably one of the reasons why the research at Denisova is so internationalized. New technological breakthroughs have changed things quite a lot in recent history, though.

One example is something called Zooarcheology by mass spectrometry, commonly abbreviated as ZooMs. This technology was developed at

Manchester University by Mike Buckley and his colleagues based on breakthroughs in food science research. ZooMs are used for studies based on collagen samples, which are proteins that are found in bones and can be preserved for hundreds of thousands of years, depending on the conditions to which fossil remains are exposed. Mammals or, more precisely, mammal groups each carry their unique collagen types, which ZooMs can read and use to identify the species.

According to Higham and Katerina Douka of the Max Planck Institute, this technology greatly speeds up their work because it allows them to quickly identify which bones are of animal origin and which come from humans. After this initial classification, researchers can do some finer, more diligent genetic work. We will detail the research conducted on some of the most important fossils from the cave in one of the later chapters.

Geographic and Climate Conditions Around Denisova

To this day, much of the region around the Altai Mountains remains naturally pristine and diverse.

For millennia, today's Altai Krai and the wider Siberian range around it have been home to countless species apart from different hominins. These lands are still brimming with life and are renowned and cherished for their biodiversity, just like Siberia, in general. The Altai mountain range consists of numerous mountains and smaller mountain ranges, some of which are quite imposing, to say the least. The highest Altai mountain is the Belukha Mountain, which reaches an elevation of 14,783 ft (4,506 m) at its highest peak. Other notably high mountains in the Altai range include Monkh Khairkhan, Sutai, Tsambagarav, all of which are in Mongolia and Khuiten, which China and Mongolia share. Belukha, on the other hand, is split between Russia and Kazakhstan.

There are also various lakes throughout the region in the countries that converge here, some of which are rather large. Naturally, some of these lakes are situated at considerable altitudes, like the saline lake of Uvs at around 2,490 ft (759 m) or Khar at around 3,715 ft (1,132 m). Other prominent lakes in the region include the Khyargas, Dorgon, and other smaller lakes.

Furthermore, the region also includes a few plateaus and valleys at various altitudes, such as the Katun, Charysh, Uba, Ulba, and Bukhtarma valleys. These valleys are usually formed around local rivers that carry the same names, as is often the case elsewhere in the world. Ob, a major Russian river flows through the region and is formed where Katun and Biya join.

Needless to say, the Altai mountain range is a rugged region with a very diverse configuration. Apart from the climate, such geography has impacted the development of incredible biodiversity of flora and fauna. It has also dictated the way of life for many people who have inhabited the region through the ages. The interesting thing about the climate is how little it has changed since the last ice age, which has allowed for the local fauna to remain the same in large part, save for a few species that have gone extinct, such as mammoths.

You will learn quite a bit about the history of human settlement in this region, but today's Russian Altai Krai is relatively ethnically homogeneous. Today, the entire federal subject is inhabited by around 2.4 million people, which is a significant reduction compared to a population of 2.8 million in 1989. More than 90% of these locals are Russians, while Germans, perhaps somewhat unexpectedly, form around 2.1%. Smaller minorities include Ukrainians, Kazakhs, Tatars, Armenians, and others. Russian history in the Altai region generally starts around the 18th century. This was a time when runaways of all sorts, religious and otherwise, came to the region and started to inhabit what was originally Chinese territory. These lands eventually came under Russian sovereignty in 1869, and the country began a process of colonization after that point.

The Field of Paleoanthropology

Along with genetics, paleoanthropology is one of the main scientific disciplines helping us unlock the secrets of what we have found. Simply put, paleoanthropology is the branch of anthropology that primarily focuses on studying hominid fossils. Anthropology itself is, of course, the study of human culture and development, including biological, physiological, and evolutionary. In essence, it is the study of humanity.

In a narrower sense, paleoanthropology also focuses on determining how, why, and when anatomically modern humans developed, which paleoanthropologists often refer to as hominization. One of the main ways these things are studied is through understanding the relationships and affinities among different evolutionary branches of the human family tree within the Hominidae taxonomic family of primates, commonly split into great apes and hominids.

The most important forms of evidence giving us clues into these things can be classified into biological and cultural evidence. The former includes all those remains, such as bones, fragments, and traces, which can be used for DNA extraction and other research. On the other hand, cultural evidence generally revolves around prehistoric tools and various other artifacts, as well as the remains of settlements. As such, archeology plays a major role in this arena.

As a science, paleoanthropology can perhaps trace its roots to the 18th century which was the first time when our own species was called *Homo sapiens*. This happened in 1758 when Carl Linnaeus published a new edition of his *Systema Naturae*. At this time, experts already saw great apes and us as closely related, especially chimpanzees. Based on morphological similarities and natural range alone, these early paleoanthropologists were able to conclude that humans, chimps, and gorillas shared a common ancestor whose fossils should be looked for in Africa.

These were the early days of human taxonomic classification, and paleoanthropology would be solidified as a science around the late 19th century as the study of human evolution sped up. Early paleoanthropology was shaped by monumental published works such as *Evidence as to Man's Place in Nature and The Descent of Man* by Thomas Huxley and Charles Darwin, respectively. The discovery of the first Neanderthal remains around the half of the 19th century was also crucial.

This was when paleoanthropology more-or-less began and was then cemented as a field of study by the aforementioned publications. Darwin's famous On the Origin of Species, which was published in 1859, was another crucial milestone because it formalized the idea of biological evolution. No longer were the assumptions of human evolution based primarily on creatures' physical appearance but on science and concrete theories.

By the 21st century, paleoanthropologists had made incredible discoveries, and our knowledge about human evolution is now miles ahead of those early speculations. Thus far, the century has been marked by a variety of newly discovered species, some of which include Australopithecus sediba, Homo naledi, Orrorin tugenensis *Ardipithecus kadabba,* and *Australopithecus deyiremeda.* The fossil remains of all these species were found and identified across the African continent.

Chapter Two:

The Human Family

I t is no secret that we have once coexisted with other human species, notably the Neanderthals. There are indications of other species and sub-species that the ancestors of archaic humans might have branched off into, but Neanderthals are the ones we've traditionally known the most about, as well as the most recently extinct. With the discovery of Denisovans and the growing pool of knowledge that we have accumulated about these archaic cousins of ours, all of this has begun to change. Still, understanding the basics of how our species evolved and split off into its own branch is important for putting things in perspective and knowing what to do with the information we gather.

Human Evolution

The evolutionary process that led to the emergence of anatomically modern humans *(Homo sapiens)* was a very complex process that took millions of years of natural selection and competition. Much of it is unclear, and, rather famously, there are still some missing links. Still, the process can be summed up and relatively simplified for easier understanding that puts things in perspective and gives us a solid idea of roughly when and how we showed up on the scene.

Human evolution is generally traced to a beginning some ten to twelve million years ago when ancestral primates split off into two groups from a common ancestor, eventually leading to the emergence of the species we know today. The first of the two groups retained an arboreal lifestyle (living mostly in trees) for the most part and continued inhabiting primarily jungles and other densely forested areas. The early members of this group were the ancestors of most of the species we now consider as of great apes, including such examples as gorillas, chimps, and orangutans.

The other group became distinct when it turned mostly terrestrial, meaning that they adapted to living on and exploring the grounds. Another important aspect of their evolution was that they became bipedal (walking on two legs) as opposed to their cousins, who remained quadrupeds, which we see to this day in apes. These evolved terrestrial primates eventually gave rise to a genus known as Homo, which descended from an earlier genus called *Australopithecus*. The genus *Homo* is now almost completely extinct, except for one extant species–*Homo sapiens*, which is our species.

Other extinct species that this genus encompassed are all either ancestral or just closely related to us, including the very important *Homo erectus*. This is one of the first identified species in the *Homo genus* and is our ancestor, emerging some 2 million years ago. Another example of a Homo species, which is not our ancestor but a relative, would be *Homo neanderthalensis*, commonly known as Neanderthals.

Homo erectus was probably the first human ancestor who started using fire, and they eventually began to migrate from Africa and spread into Europe. As they moved around and adapted, new species began to form and are today identified as such by paleoanthropology. These early hominins were hunter-gatherers, which was the main motivation for them to move and spread out all over the African continent before moving into Eurasia. Some of the most important new species began to emerge from Homo erectus some 500,000 years ago, beginning the crucial processes for the eventual evolution of our species. Apart from Neanderthals, another example of a non-ancestral but related species, as we know thanks to discoveries in southern Russia, were the Denisovans.

As for us, paleoanthropology generally dates our beginnings to some 2-300,000 years ago when the first anatomically modern humans are believed to have emerged. Traditionally, our species' emergence from the *Homo erectus* genus was believed to have occurred in Africa, which is still the predominant theory. According to this view, our species began to migrate out of Africa in waves from 250,000 to 130,000 years ago. By 50,000 years ago, Eurasia and Oceania were thoroughly settled. As they moved around, our early *Homo sapiens* ancestors met and interbred with those other descendants of *Homo erectus*, such as Neanderthals and possibly others. At the same time, Neanderthals did the same with other non-sapiens like the main actors in our book, the Denisovans.

Neanderthals

Neanderthals are perhaps the most famous archaic people that we know of, at least by name. Unfortunately, not many people know much about Neanderthals, and it's not uncommon for them to hold misconceptions such as that Neanderthals were our direct ancestors. In fact, these extinct archaic humans were a whole other species or subspecies that lived alongside us and eventually disappeared. However, before they went extinct, Neanderthals certainly left their trace both in the physical evidence that they left behind and the genetic legacy that we now carry.

Neanderthals went extinct relatively recently, around 40,000 years ago, after having lived and thrived all over Eurasia. The reason for their extinction is still the object of a lot of debate and research, with numerous factors suggested, ranging from climate change to pandemics. It's also possible that we might have contributed to their extinction, but it's unknown to what degree. What's certain is that early modern humans from Europe eventually outbred and outcompeted Neanderthals in every way, which led to their complete replacement.

These archaic humans got their name from the location where the first Neanderthal was found, the Neander Valley in what is now Germany. The initial specimen, now called simply Neanderthal 1, was found here in 1856 and was initially met with quite a bit of skepticism. At first, many anthropologists called the legitimacy of these remains into question, but they were eventually confirmed as authentic. Researchers also initially believed that Neanderthals were a lot more primitive and less developed than they actually were.

It's still uncertain whether Neanderthals mastered fire, but we know that they were quite adept at making some rather sophisticated stone tools, also known as the Mousterian industry. Subsequent discoveries and research have indicated that Neanderthals were likely capable of a very wide range of other skills and technologies. Evidence suggests that Neanderthals were able to make simple clothing garments, weave, navigate the Mediterranean, engage in primitive medicine, roast or cook food, make adhesive tar, improve their cave dwellings with hearths, and much more.

Some paleoanthropologists also believe that Neanderthals engaged in quite a lot of cave painting and other Paleolithic art, in addition to making various ornate items and primitive jewelry. Other suggestions have concerned the possibility that Neanderthals were religious and linguistically articulate, although there have been no sufficient indications as to the complexity of their supposed language. These things haven't been confirmed beyond a reasonable doubt yet, but Neanderthal physical evidence stretches far and wide across Eurasia, with a constant possibility that new discoveries will emerge.

In regard to physical appearance, these hominins were similar to our ancestors and us, of course, but with some important differences. In proportion to their bodies, Neanderthal limbs were shorter, which might have been the result of their distribution in cold climates. Neanderthals had other cold-climate adaptations as well, which made them well-suited for Eurasian grounds at that time.

Other Species and Early Modern Humans

Early modern human (EMH), also referred to as anatomically modern human (AMH), is a way in which paleoanthropologists refer to those *Homo sapiens* that first had physical features that we now see in contemporary humans. This is a way to ensure they aren't confused with other archaic human species, especially when the topic of discussion is Homo species that lived together, such as in Europe.

As far as actual physical evidence of our direct ancestors and relatives is concerned, we have a few very old *Homo sapiens* discoveries that we can rely on, which are the oldest people we know. These include such discoveries as Omo-Kibish I, Florisbad, and Jabel Irhoud, which date back to around 196,000, 259,000, and 300,000 years, respectively. Among all the species of the genus Homo, the oldest individual we have found was discovered by Louis Leakey and his colleagues in 1964. This was the *Homo habilis*, also colloquially known as the handyman, the first uncovered *Homo* confirmed to have used stone tools. This old species was a *Homo* branch of its own, just like *Homo erectus*. It evolved around 2 million years ago and went extinct some 500,000 years after that. The date of the evolution and extinction of such species of *Homo* puts things in perspective for us and illustrates how relatively recently we have entered the evolutionary scene.

As for *H. erectus*, the first fossil remains were found in 1891 in Asia by Eugene Dubois. The two finest specimens we have are Pithecanthropus and Sinanthropus, also known as the ape-man and Chinese-man, respectively. Having evolved some 1.8 million years ago, H. erectus eventually left East Africa and ended up in Asia, where their use of stone tools was first documented. Even these distant ancestors of ours were most likely capable of using and understanding various symbols. Paleoanthropologists have concluded this based on shells that Dubois brought to Europe after having found them in Java. These engraved shells, a sign of prehistoric creativity, are most likely between 430,000 and 540,000 years old.

Denisovans themselves come into the picture outside of Africa, just like Neanderthals, at least as far as we know based on current evidence. They are related to Neanderthals and have likely evolved from the same ancestor known as Neandersovans, who went extinct some 300,000 years ago. These Neandersovans and Homo sapiens likely started to gradually split off from the same branch around half a million years ago. The former, including Neanderthals, is considered the European branch while *H. sapiens* is the African branch. As such, despite common ancestry that ultimately goes back to *H. erectus* and Australopithecus before them, it's clear that our species had quite a different evolutionary path than Neanderthals and Denisovans.

Early Modern Humans and Neanderthals

Although they evolved on different continents, *H. sapiens* and *H. neanderthalensis* most likely showed up around the same time. While our species slowly made its way across Africa in the initial migrations, Neanderthals prowled Europe and Asia's landscapes. As our species began to make its way into Europe in waves, the eventual encounter and interaction with Neanderthals became unavoidable. This is despite the fact that Neanderthals were rather thinly dispersed for most of their existence. *H. sapiens*, on the other hand, proved to be rather successful in settling and colonizing the new continental mass.

The exact manner and trajectory of those migrations out of Africa is, of course, something that's still being researched and debated. For example, a long-standing discussion concerns the final range of *H. sapiens* within Africa itself. Some experts theorize that the species had reached every corner of Africa before venturing beyond the continent, while others disagree. Evidence to support the former has been found in Morocco, for instance.

There are also various bits of evidence that gave us insight into where and when our ancestors moved as they left Africa. For instance, we have solid evidence suggesting that our species was already living in today's Israel around 180,000 years ago. What this means is that we probably didn't go straight from Africa to Europe but instead made stops along the way, lasting tens of thousands of years. We may find older specimens eventually, but as of right now, 45,000 years ago was when H. sapiens is confirmed to have settled in Europe.

By the time we made it to the old continent, Neanderthals were distributed far and wide. We don't know that much about how exactly these two species interacted, but we do know for a fact that they interbred. Contemporary Europeans and Asians generally carry some 1 to 4% of Neanderthal and Denisovan DNA.

Both Neanderthals and EMHs showed a propensity for creativity, making things not just for utility but also aesthetic pursuits resembling primitive art. Cave wall paintings attributed to *H. sapiens* have been identified and dated 36,000 or more years ago. Multiple discoveries of such art have shown us that these ancestors of ours were already very sophisticated and artistic, testifying to their advanced development. Despite that, there is no evidence to suggest that we played a significant role in the extinction of Neanderthals. Neanderthal populations were frequently rather small, which made it easier for harmful genes to be persistently passed on. Even though these hominins showed signs of developing regional cultures, there was no significant interconnection and communication. It's entirely possible that *H. sapiens* simply outbred and replaced a species that was already on its way out, especially due to climate change.

Chapter Three:

The Discoveries at Denisova

I n total, fossil remains have allowed researchers to identify four separate Denisovan individuals so far. In one of the most unexpected discoveries on top of that, anthropologists have also isolated the remains of one individual born from a Denisovan father and a Neanderthal mother. In addition, research at Denisova has also identified numerous other individuals who were solely Neanderthal. The discovery of a mixed individual has been one of the most important findings on locale, given the scarcity of evidence and the low number of individuals that have been successfully identified.

This suggests that such mixing was relatively common whenever the different human species or sub-species met, and the region around Denisova seems to have been the site of many such meetings and interactions. Apart from these genetic exchanges, we can also assume with a fair amount of certainty that Denisovans interacted with other humans in other ways and perhaps closely coexisted in some instances. DNA studies have also shown that Denisovans interbred with another branch of archaic humans other than Neanderthals and the direct ancestors of Homo sapiens. These mysterious hominins are yet to be identified, but it appears that they split off into separate species or sub-species some 1,000,000 years ago. These are only small snippets of the incredible story that we have been uncovering thanks to the traces found at Denisova.

Initial Discoveries and the Beginning of Research

The first meaningful explorations in the cave began in 1970 and would go on for decades, bringing various interesting discoveries to light. Initially, researchers mostly found indications of *Homo sapiens* and Neanderthal presence, although it was uncertain whether these two occupied the cave and the surrounding area at the same time or one after the other. Valuable finds dating to the Middle and Upper Paleolithic attracted significant attention and quickly established the Denisova Cave as a valuable archeological site.

Major discoveries that helped identify the presence of a new hominin strain on locale came later, though. The first breakthrough happened in 2008 when a group of Russian paleoanthropologists discovered a piece of a finger bone about the size of a pea. This fossil piece was initially assumed to be yet another Neanderthal or *Homo sapiens* trace. The scientists identified the bone fragment as belonging to a juvenile girl who likely died around 40,000 years ago. It wasn't clear that this bone fragment belonged to a previously unknown kind of hominin until scientists extracted and analyzed a DNA sample from the bone. This new mysterious human was soon thereafter named Denisovan after the cave.

Researchers were able to learn many fascinating things just from these DNA samples alone. The mysterious prehistoric girl was dubbed Denisova 3, and it was determined that she lived at some point between 52,000 to 76,000 years ago. The importance of this discovery was also in the light it was able to shed on previous discoveries that had puzzled paleoanthropologists since 2000. Namely, the researchers were able to learn much about this other, previously unidentified sample from the cave. The fossil in question is a molar tooth that belonged to an individual later named Denisova 4.

The Denisova Cave quickly became a hotspot of paleoanthropology research, and the findings soon became known abroad, internationalizing the research efforts. Not long after those initial discoveries, new evidence began to pop up, notably in 2010 when two more molars were found. The first of the teeth was a permanent one, and it was identified as having belonged to a male individual, whom the researchers named Denisova 8. This specimen was dated more than 100,000 years ago. The second tooth was once again left behind by a very small child, a girl who most likely lived even earlier. This child most likely lived at some point between 120,000 and 194,000 years ago.

The extraction and study of DNA samples from these fossil remains gained momentum in 2010 as a joint international effort. Russian and foreign scientists successfully sequenced a complete mitochondrial DNA genome from the 2008 samples. In short, mitochondrial DNA (as opposed to nuclear DNA) is suitable for determining the specimen's

date of origin and genetic similarity to other specimens.

The thing that initially had researchers believing that they had stumbled upon more Neanderthal fossils was that the finger bone fragment was
associated with uncovered Mousterian stone tool
artifacts. Upon DNA inspection, though, it turned
out that this DNA was much more distinct from
ours than Neanderthal DNA is. Denisovan mtD-
NA samples had roughly twice as many differences
from modern *Homo sapiens* samples. This strongly
suggests that Denisovans descended from the same
common ancestor but had branched off as a lineage
before Neanderthals and us. In the end, this valuable mtDNA evidence has pointed out that anatomically modern humans, Neanderthals, and this
third species or sub-species have called the Altai
region their home at the same time around 40,000
years ago.

Further Findings

Roughly around the time of the aforementioned
mtDNA sequencing, other researchers were busy
getting a DNA sample from the nuclei of the cells in

the same finger fragment. The samples were used to successfully sequence the nuclear genome, which revealed other valuable information. These studies confirmed the fundamental genetic differences that this new hominin had when compared to Neanderthals and us. On top of that, a tooth that the paleoanthropologists examined was very different from the teeth of regular Neanderthals and *Homo sapiens*. While comparing nuclear genomes, the geneticists also found that modern humans in Melanesia, for example, shared some 4 to 6% of genetic material with Denisovans. This information gave valuable insight into the range that Denisovans reached as well as their mingling with early modern humans.

The year 2012 brought some even more incredible discoveries. Many researchers were quite shocked by the long bone piece that turned out to have belonged to a half-Neanderthal and half-Denisovan female who lived sometime between 80,000 and 120,000 years ago. The interaction and interbreeding between *Homo sapiens* and Neanderthals, for instance, was something that we've known about for quite some time. However, the identification of a whole new human species or sub-species and such a quick confirmation that others intermingled with them really took the paleoanthropology community by storm.

As far as Neanderthals are concerned, the remains of at least two pure Neanderthals were found and studied by geneticists. Additional Neanderthal DNA was extracted from sediments, all of which gave researchers a window into the Neanderthal presence in the Denisova Cave and the surrounding area. Between roughly 193,000 and 97,000 years ago, Neanderthals called this cave their home, most likely on numerous occasions, although with prolonged periods of absence.

As for *Homo sapiens*, no concrete evidence of their presence has been found on-locale. The best we have are subtle indications in the form of artifacts that appear as though they might have been made by our species, although this couldn't be confirmed. Examples include bone arrowheads and ornamental tooth pendants that are some 49,000 years old at most. These artifacts are described as having certain characteristics reminiscent of other *Homo sapiens* creations, but this evidence is circumstantial at best. Another indication that these artifacts might have come from our species is that they are younger than the last proven Denisovan presence in the cave, but this is something that can easily change with new discoveries. No bones, fragments, or any shred of DNA has yet indicated that our ancestors ever occupied the cave in prehistory.

This doesn't hold true for other parts of this region, though, as the remains of modern humans have been identified at another site by the name of Ust'-Ishim, located northwest of the cave. A valuable fossil specimen belonging to a 45,000-year-old individual now referred to as the Ust'-Ishim man was found there in 2008. This means that while our ancestors perhaps didn't personally make any of Denisova Cave's artifacts, their cultural influence might have gradually found its way to Denisovans living there.

Other Prehistoric Discoveries at Denisova

Among other things, the Denisova Cave has been the site of the discovery of what many paleoanthropologists believe is the oldest sewing needle ever found, dating back to around 50,000 years ago. The needle was made out of bird bone and is 2.8 inches

(7 cm) long. There was another prehistoric needle found in South Africa, which some researchers have suggested might be older, but there is still no consensus on this.

In regard to Neanderthal excavations and research, one of the most important finds at Denisova was a toe bone fragment found in 2010. This fossil was confirmed to have come from a Neanderthal who was roughly the contemporary of the aforementioned Denisovan finger fragment. Once again, DNA was used to confirm the species beyond any doubt. The DNA that was extracted from this toe bone became one of the most important samples in Neanderthal genetic research. The individual who left this fossil behind was named the Altai Neanderthal and dated to some 120,000 years ago. One of the most interesting things about the Altai Neanderthal is that his nuclear genome stands out a bit among other Neanderthal nuclear DNA samples that have been extracted over the years. Furthermore, the Ust'-Ishim man and modern *Homo sapiens* are genetically more similar to other Neanderthals than they are to the Altai one. Among other possibilities, this indicates that the

Altai Neanderthals likely started to branch off from other Neanderthals before they started to intermingle with modern humans.

Another interesting discovery in the cave was that of a 32,000-year-old "horse" fossil. The species (from the Equus genus) was determined to be *Equus ovodovi*, also called the *Ovodov* horse. Remains of this long-extinct animal were also found in another cave in Russia's Republic of Khakassia, in south-central Siberia. These remains date back to around 40,000 years ago. The two fossils both yielded DNA extracts that turned out to be very similar, while the species itself genetically resembles today's zebras.

As already briefly mentioned, the Denisova Cave research has uncovered artifacts as well, quite a few of them, in fact. Apart from the artifacts we've already touched upon, archeologists have also unearthed early Middle Paleolithic (300,000 to 30,000 years ago) stone tools of various kinds. Discovered tools from this category are often based on disk-shaped cores, but other shapes such as flakes and Levallois cores were also found at Denisova. These tools came in various forms and were mostly used for scraping, as primitive saws (denticulate tools), and other purposes. Such tools were found in all the cave's chambers.

The archaic folks who inhabited Denisova continued using similar tools through the middle of the Middle Paleolithic, with some additional innovations. Judging by the presence of burins and other primitive chisel-type tools, Denisovans were interested in carving and engraving wood and bones for various purposes. Various artifacts that originate in the early Upper Paleolithic (50,000 to 12,000 years ago) were also found throughout the cave. This category of Denisova artifacts includes more blades and Levallois-core tools, in addition to many previously used technologies. Blades were undoubtedly more advanced during this time, however, especially starting some 36,000 years ago.

In the Upper Paleolithic category, archeologists also found various bone tools and relatively simple ornaments made of a range of materials. Rings, pendants, bracelets, and other similar "jewelry" were mostly made from ivory, bone, animal teeth, but also from marble. Of course, as discussed, Denisovans were mostly gone in the Upper Paleolithic period, at least from Denisova, so it isn't certain who left these tools and ornaments behind.

The Upper Paleolithic was a time when our species was already moving into Siberia, so the artifacts in this layer could have been brought in by Neanderthals who either acquired them from sapiens or made them based on cultural exchange. This is a likely scenario because there are no fossils or genetic traces of our species in this region during that time.

All in all, the Denisova Cave is a treasure trove of hints, bits, and pieces that archeologists and paleoanthropologists will continue to scour for a long time to come. We may learn that Denisovans persisted for longer than we thought or that our direct ancestors did, in fact, visit them in these parts, but we simply can't confirm these things as of right now.

Chapter Four:

Denny

The aforementioned Neanderthal-Denisovan hybrid that was found in 2012 was undoubtedly one of the fascinating discoveries so far. It's also perhaps the discovery that has garnered the most attention with continuous efforts to reconstruct what this girl might have been like, both physically and behaviorally. Some most distinguished experts leading the efforts to unlock this specimen's secrets, especially in the early stage, were paleo-geneticists Svante Paabo and Viviane Slon at the Max Planck Institute for Evolutionary Anthropology, located in Leipzig, Germany. Numerous theories have cropped up, and quite a few experts have offered their views too. This chapter will go into a bit more detail about this monumental discovery and its implications.

Denisovan 11, commonly named Denny, lived at some point between 80,000 and 120,000 years ago, although a relative consensus generally hovers around 90,000 years. These findings were the result of studies conducted in 2016 to determine the specimen's age and when the individual died. This female hominin was most likely no less than 13 years of age but almost certainly juvenile, and that's taking into account what we have been able to determine about the average height of Denisovans and Neanderthals alike.

The importance of Denny's discovery extends well beyond the efforts just to understand Denisovans or Neanderthals. Just a couple of years after the new Denisovan species was discovered, fate would have it that Denny would be the first prehistoric specimen that we've ever found to be the offspring of two distinct human species or sub-species. In Denny's case, as mentioned earlier, the father was Denisovan and the mother Neanderthal. There have been bits of evidence and indications of breeding (such as our own genes) between different human species before, but we've never had an offspring specimen to confirm one such instance before.

In that regard, Denny is quite unprecedented in paleoanthropology. This has many important implications in the field of human genetic study. For one, we can now find out more when running comparisons on extracted genomes from different human species. By using Denny's sample as a reference, we can get a better idea of just how often different hominin species interbred and what this might mean for us today.

Another important implication concerns the manner in which Neanderthals and Denisovans have gone extinct. For quite some time, certain paleoanthropologists have been suggesting that neither of the two species actually went extinct but were instead bred out and assimilated by *Homo sapiens*. Denny's existence certainly doesn't prove such theories beyond a reasonable doubt, but it does lend additional credence to them and has at least brought them back into public discourse. Denny has confirmed for us, concerning Neanderthals, that they were migrating from Western Europe to Central Eurasia for a long time before their extinctions, possibly tens of thousands of years. Geneticists determined this by uncovering that Denny's mom's DNA shared a greater affinity with Western European Neanderthal DNA than with those Neanderthals who lived around Denisova.

Research and Identification

As usual, the fossil itself is very small and is little more than a bone fragment shorter than one inch. Denny's sample bone fragment was given the code DC1227 to identify it, apart from its other name of Denisova 11. Despite everything that we have learned thanks to DNA extraction, researchers remain unsure which part of the body the fragment came from, although it was likely either from a leg or an arm. In the process of DNA extraction, a tiny piece of the fragment had to be taken off, which reduced the fossil's original size. When it was first found, Denny's fragment was exactly 0.97 by 0.33 inches or 24.7 by 8.39 millimeters.

Russians initially found the sample in 2012 in the eastern chamber or gallery of the Denisova Cave. Unsure of the fragment's origins, but probably operating on the assumption that it belonged to Neanderthals like most other fossils there, the archeologists stored the sample away with thousands of other fragments that were recovered on locale but unidentified. As foreign scientists were already participating in the excavations and studies in the cave, the fragment initially found its way to the desk of Samantha Brown, University of Oxford, in 2016. Brown was tasked with analyzing a great many such fragments to determine which animals they belonged to. Of course, Brown soon realized that this particular piece of bone belonged to some sort of hominin, which was also when she determined roughly how old the evidence was.

This was when the sample was shown to experts from the Max Planck Institute for Evolutionary Anthropology, including Katerina Douka, given their experience with Denisovan DNA research. Researchers at the institute conducted both mitochondrial and nuclear DNA testing and finalized their research by 2018. During that year, the results were published and hailed as one of the most important discoveries in paleoanthropology in a very long time. Researchers around the world could now get a much better insight into how different prehistoric hominins interacted and interbred. The discoveries were praised throughout the scientific community in prestigious institutions like Harvard Medical School.

Douka later described how much material she and her colleagues had to work with initially. When they got in contact with their Russian peers, among them Mikhail Shunkov and Anatoly Derevyanko, they were simply given a bag full of unsorted bone fragments. These samples were considered to be next to identifiable.

The first step was to separate each bone fragment and take out a small, 20-mg sample that would be used to identify the source. These tiny samples were then placed in individual test tubes, each with its unique mark. This process alone took around three months, at which point the team managed to separate and prepare 150 individual samples. According to Higham, however, the researchers needed many more samples. The scope of the work required more scientists, so Higham started looking for volunteers among postgraduate students. Despite the fascinating, groundbreaking work they were doing, nobody volunteered for two weeks. Eventually, though, Higham was approached by Samantha Brown, who sought to participate in the research while working on her master's dissertation, and that's how she ended up working on this project.

From that point on, Brown began working on the same part of the job, preparing and labeling samples for weeks to come. In the course of this phase, Brown prepared around 700 samples, all neatly marked and organized. These samples were analyzed in a laboratory in Manchester, where analysts determined that many of the bone fragments belonged to animals like cows, among other species. Unfortunately, there wasn't a single human bone fragment among all the samples.

Although disappointed, Samantha Brown wouldn't let herself be dissuaded by this setback, and she continued preparing many other samples and having them analyzed. Higham later praised her diligence, stating that she helped prepare another 1,500 samples for the Manchester lab. The team's persistence paid off when lab specialists determined that at least one fragment had human origins, although it was yet to be determined what exact species and era it was from. Even though this was only confirmation that the sample belonged to a hominin in the broadest sense, it was proof that their techniques worked and their efforts paid off, which made the team very excited.

Unfortunately, this was when the capabilities of ZooMs reached their limit, as the technology could not be used to determine the exact species that had left the bone fragment behind. As far as the researchers knew at this point, the sample could have belonged to any great ape, Neanderthal, Denisovan, or Homo sapiens. Still, the researchers knew, based on other studies and evidence, that great apes never lived in the area around the Denisova Cave, so they could at least safely assume that the fragment had belonged to some sort of human.

As such, the next step was to determine these fine details, and this was where the Max Planck Institute came into the picture. The leading expert who received the sample was Svante Paabo because of his team's previous experience with DNA sequencing from samples found at Denisova. The geneticists soon started to uncover all various details, starting with the sample's age and the individual who left it behind.

Upon further inspection, the truth finally began to come into focus, as the researchers realized that half the DNA was Neanderthal and the other half Denisovan. Paabo and his team initially chalked this up to some sort of mistake, most likely contamination of the sample. They proceeded to repeat the test, and this time there was no mistaking it: they were dealing with the remains of a 90,000-year-old human hybrid. And so, the first confirmed hybrid made up of two hominin species was identified and named Denny.

Other Revelations

After determining Denny's hybrid nature, researchers started taking a closer look at her parents' DNA. As it turned out, Denny's Denisovan father already had traces of Neanderthal DNA, suggesting that the conception of Denny was certainly not the first time the two species interbred. One might be forgiven for taking this as a sign that interbreeding between Denisovans and Neanderthals was commonplace, but Douka and other scientists on the project have argued against this. There is simply too much clear distinction between Denisovan and Neanderthal DNA, in general, to assume that they interbred on a regular basis.

That interbreeding occurred among different human species from time to time has never really been a secret, though. However, one of the key questions is why Neanderthals and Denisovans seem to have intermingled exclusively around Denisova. Of course, it's always possible that this is simply wrong and that we just haven't found evidence of intermingling elsewhere – evidence that we might indeed find at some point.

Paleoanthropologists have offered a potential explanation that might give us concrete answers, though. One theory suggests that the Denisova Cave was simply situated in what could be seen as a sort of borderland between the two species. As such, it would have been positioned at the eastern edge of the Neanderthal range and the western edge of the Denisovan range. Members of these European and eastern species would have both wanted to occupy the cave from time to time since it has always provided quality natural shelter. In that regard, the cave could be seen as a sort of prehistoric border outpost, serving as a point of occasional contact.

This theory emerged from the findings that the researchers made while studying Denny's Neanderthal mother's DNA. These studies showed that Denny's mom most likely came from the Balkan region of southeast Europe, at least by ancestry. This Neanderthal woman's not-so-distant ancestors

were likely the ones who migrated to these out-
er regions of the historical Neanderthal range in
Eurasia. This was where Denny's mother eventually ran into her Denisovan mate, whose ancestors
also likely migrated to the area around Denisova at
some point.

That's just a theory so far, though, and not
the strongest one at that. It's what some evidence
points to, but we still have so much more to dis-
cover and learn. As of now, we just can't confirm
whether Denisovans lived only to the east of Denisova, although their genetic traces in eastern regions point to that possibility. To determine these
things, researchers will have to get their hands on
new samples from other locations.

Interestingly enough, Higham and other colleagues have suggested that such evidence might
have already been discovered but misidentified and
wrongly labeled. The problem is in the fact that
many of the samples that the researchers suspect
might be Denisovan are now in museums, which
makes it difficult to obtain them for studies.

These and other paleoanthropologists have
long had their sights on parts of eastern Russia,

China, and Southeast Asia. According to Douka and Higham, one of their goals is to collaborate with Chinese experts and their laboratories. In the absence of direct collaboration, just transferring ZooMs technology to these Chinese labs could be a major step for research efforts, in general. The idea is to get this technology over to the Chinese so that they could quickly sort through the fragments that they have and set aside the human remains. After that, all sorts of collaboration in genetic research could yield new and unprecedented discoveries.

Chapter Five:

Other Denisovan Characteristics and Evidence

As you can see, there's plenty we can learn about Denisovans, but there are still many mysteries surrounding them. This is no surprise, given their relatively recent discovery and identification as a species or sub-species. However, not all the discoveries surrounding Denisovans have been all that recent. Some bits of evidence were discovered quite a while ago, but were simply unidentified until recently. In this chapter, we will try to piece together what little information we have about the Denisovans' physical appearance and characteristics while also taking a look at some other fascinating evidence and locations that are of interest to paleoanthropology.

Appearance and Additional Findings

The DNA and mtDNA genomes that have been sequenced from Denisovan samples have clearly given us a lot of invaluable insight into who these mysterious cousins were. Unfortunately, there is a lot we don't know about Denisovans on the physical side of things. We can't reconstruct their faces and bodies in a lot of meaningful detail yet, but we have been able to learn a thing or two about their skeletal traits, both from the DNA samples and the fossils themselves.

As we briefly mentioned earlier, the Denisovans' teeth were significantly different from those of sapiens and Neanderthals. Their teeth were big, strong, and robust, much more alike the teeth of *Homo erectus* than ours are. Among Denisovans, Neanderthals, and modern humans, we have the smallest teeth, but even those of Neanderthals were significantly smaller than Denisovans'. These teeth have been one of the first physical traits that we have been able to identify as uniquely Denisovan. As time goes on and we hopefully find more Denisovan remains elsewhere across Eurasia, we might make new discoveries, but so far, we know for a fact that these teeth were a typical feature of Altai Denisovans.

Like most human or animal species out there, Denisovans likely had quite a bit of variety among different individuals when it came to appearance and various physical features. Still, DNA evidence suggests that some typical features were widespread, including relatively dark skin combined with brown eyes and hair that was usually dark or brown. It's also important to consider that there is a strong possibility that Denisovans were spread out over a significantly wider range than we can currently confirm, so it's even more difficult to generalize their physical features yet.

The conclusions we have drawn about the teeth of Denisovans are based partly on the uncovered tooth fossils that we've mentioned, but there was another crucial discovery that has told us quite a lot. Namely, a certain human jawbone was found in the Baishiya Karst cave in Tibet and eventually identified as Denisovan. This fossil is also known as the Xiahe mandible. This particular fossil dates back to about 160,000 years ago and clearly shows the remains of what was once a very strong jaw with powerful teeth.

The Xiahe Mandible

This jaw fragment suggests certain similarities between earlier Denisovans and some more primitive

Neanderthals. The location of the fossil in Tibet also tells us something about the range of Denisovans, as well as the fact that they lived at high altitudes. This meant that they had certain high-altitude adaptations that might have been passed on genetically to Sherpas, a Tibetan ethnic group that numbers more than 500,000 people today.

The jawbone fossil was another piece of evidence that the Max Planck Institute studied for Evolutionary Anthropology. One of the institute's leading researchers on this fossil, Jean-Jacques Hublin, explained that the Baishiya Karst jawbone was a monumental discovery, particularly because it showed that archaic humans could live at very high altitudes, which was previously doubtful. Based on the information that the researchers gathered while trying to determine how old this fossil was, we also learned other interesting things about the location these Denisovans lived on.

For example, the dating of the fossil shows us that these archaic humans lived in this region when the climate was significantly colder and harsher than today. Temperatures would routinely drop down to -22 °F (-30 °C), which is difficult to deal with anywhere, let alone at an altitude of more than 10,000 feet. Even with all our modern clothes and other protection, these temperatures are considered extreme. The fact that these archaic, primitive hominins could survive for so long in such conditions is fascinating, to say the least.

As for the fossil itself, this mandible was named after the Chinese Xiahe County, located on the Tibetan Plateau. This was the first time a Denisovan fossil was discovered somewhere other than the Denisova Cave, and, as such, it was a major victory for paleoanthropology. On top of that, the Xiahe mandible is the largest and most complete Denisovan fossil to date. The discovery of this evidence was far more accidental than most of the findings in Russia, too.

Namely, the mandible was discovered back in 1980 by a Tibetan Buddhist monk who came to the Baishiya Karst Cave to meditate. He noticed that the remains were human, and he informed a Buddhist custodian by the name of Jigme Tenpe Wangchug, who immediately recognized that the old bone might have a great scientific value. Jigme made sure that the fossil found its way to a qualified expert, and the mandible eventually ended up in the hands of one Dong Guangrong, a geologist from Lanzhou University, an important research university in the Gansu province. Guangrong was very interested in this fossil, and he elicited the help of one of his colleagues, Chen Fahu, in studying the specimen. The two scientists were geologists above all, though, so there was only so much they could do. The specimen thus remained unclassified and unidentified for quite a while since the 1980s.

In the wake of new discoveries in paleoanthropology, Chinese scientists started studying the mandible again in 2010. Chen, Dong, and one of Chen's Ph. D. students by the name of Zhang Dongju came together and resumed their studies on the fossil while also searching numerous caves in Xiahe. At this time, the researchers weren't even sure where exactly the mandible came from. The specimen sat around for a long time, largely forgotten, so there was a lot of catching up to do, and it took years for the scientists even to determine that the jawbone came from the Baishiya Karst Cave. Once they ascertained the mandible's origin, the research team ran into other problems and delays since the cave in question is a Buddhist holy place. This meant that they had to acquire certain permits even to begin further excavations.

In 2018, the team finally acquired all the necessary papers, and the work could begin. Upon conducting a thorough survey of the entire Baishiya Karst Cave, the researchers found a range of new fossils such as animal bones as well as various artifacts, including an array of Paleolithic tools. After this survey, the Chinese scientists got in touch with the Max Planck Institute, and that's when Jean-Jacques Hublin entered the project. He employed his own Ph. D. student, one Frido Welker, and the mandible was soon identified as Denisovan.

Unlike previous Denisovan fossils found in the Altai Mountains, the Xiahe mandible has proven to be a poor source of DNA samples, so the bone was identified as Denisovan based on protein extracts. They extracted the protein sample from one of the molars that are still attached to the jawbone, of which there are actually two. The mandible itself is not an entire lower jaw, but roughly the right half of one. DNA extracts can tell us much more, but protein samples are certainly enough to confirm without any doubt that this fossil is of Denisovan origin.

This was when the researchers found out how the local Sherpas came to possess traces of Denisovan DNA. Since the long-gone Denisovans had clearly adapted to live at these high altitudes and cope with the scarcity of oxygen there, it would appear that this adaptation carried over to Sherpas, who show an impressive ability to withstand hypoxia a lack of oxygen in tissues. This would possibly mean that this population of modern humans, which occupies this particular territory to this very day, was improved and made stronger by a Denisovan gene that their early modern human ancestors had absorbed tens of thousands of years ago.

This incredible discovery tells an amazing story while, at the same time, posing various questions. As Hublin put it, the strange thing is that the Denisova Cave was at a significantly lower altitude. This has led to a couple of theories trying to explain the aforementioned gene's purpose in Denisovans themselves. One possible explanation is that this gene helped Denisovans simply achieve a higher physical endurance, in general. Yet another explanation, though, is that this was a gene that originated specifically in these high-altitude Denisovans who were better suited for such an environment than Altai Denisovans. Unfortunately, the failure to extract viable DNA samples from the Xiahe mandible has made it difficult to answer these and numerous other questions.

The discovery and successful identification of the Xiahe mandible have been unprecedented in that it is now the oldest known remain of a high-altitude human by far. Prior to this discovery, the oldest such example was Nwya Devu, another archeological site on the Tibetan Plateau, which is about 120,000 years younger than the Baishiya Karst Cave evidence. On top of that, this was the first time researchers have managed to identify an archaic hominin based only on protein samples.

Baishiya Karst Cave

As for the Baishiya Karst Cave itself, it is a Buddhist sanctuary that is situated on the northeast end of the Tibetan Plateau in the Xiahe County of the Gansu province of the People's Republic of China. Based on the aforementioned findings, this cave has been visited and used for shelter for at least 160,000 years, based on the evidence we've learned about thus far. What's certain is that this is the site of the oldest archaic human traces found on the Tibetan Plateau by far.

The cave is located at an altitude of 10,761 ft (3,280 m) above sea level, and its name suggests its nature. Namely, this is a karst cave, a cave formed from rocks like dolomite, limestone, or gypsum. This is the most common type of cave, and it occurs all over the world, with many existing examples. A cave-like this will usually form over several geological epochs thanks to acidic underground waters that seep through cracks and natural crevices and gradually wear the rocks down. Given a long enough period, openings can expand quite a bit and create spectacular cave systems. It's not uncommon for such caves to have all sorts of interesting formations within them, including various columns and shapes that can be quite peculiar in appearance.

The Baishiya Cave is around 3,280 ft (1 km) long, 66 ft (20 m) wide, and 33 ft (10 m) high, which makes it quite an imposing cave formation that's much larger than Denisova. Its length means that the interior of the cave is prone to temperature variations. The first 260 ft from the cave entrance is very habitable, which especially shows during winter. Winters can be very harsh on the Tibetan Plateau, yet the cave can maintain a temperature of around 46-48 °F (8-9 °C) during the day in winter. The cave's location is on the south side of Daliji-ashan Mountain, in the Ganjia Basin. This is also where the mouth of the Jiangla River is located, which is a tributary of the Yangqu.

The religious significance for the local Tibetan Buddhists is considerable. The cave is located just north of the Baishiya Temple, whose monks routinely visit the cave to meditate and engage in other spiritual activities. The cave also attracts Buddhist pilgrims from far and wide, not just locals. Being a naturally impressive cave with a lot of history, the Baishiya is also popular with tourists of all sorts and origins. The cave's great length has also been the object of wonder for generations, which has spawned a few local legends. One popular legend suggests that the cave is actually 31 miles (50 km) long, reaching the Chinese Qinghair province.

This has never been scientifically substantiated, of course, but the existence of such legends testifies to human curiosity and attempts to explore the cave's great depths.

Chapter Six:

An Archaic People

Denisovans are clearly a fascinating discovery with lots of potential for future research. Researchers worldwide are making great efforts to determine more about what these archaic humans looked like, where exactly they lived, how they migrated, and much else. They were certainly primitive from today's standpoint, but as you have read thus far, Denisovans and Neanderthals both lived during a time when semblances of culture and creativity began to emerge among humans of all sorts. As such, we can be certain that we will learn a lot more about these distant cousins of ours in the future.

The combination of a scarcity of evidence and the grand implications of that evidence has led to numerous interesting theories and discussions among scholars and researchers of different scientific backgrounds all over the world. There are speculations, assertions, suggestions, ideas, and theories; some backed up better than others by evidence.

You have already learned quite a few things that we know or think we know about Denisovans, but in this chapter, we will go into a bit more detail about the various characteristics and aspects of this human species.

Demographics

Determining the exact geographical range of Denisovans is something that paleoanthropologists have been working on for a while. As you have learned, Denisovans had reached well beyond the Altai Mountains. So far, Denisovan fossils have been discovered only at the two locales we discussed: the Denisova Cave and the Baishiya Karst Cave.

Thanks to the DNA that geneticists have been able to extract from those fossils, researchers could look for DNA matches all over the world. These sorts of studies eventually gave us insight into the wider Denisovan range, based on genetic traces they have left in the gene pool of today's populations. The presence of Denisovans across East Asia is more-or-less confirmed, while it's also possible that they reached western Eurasia.

DNA research has led to the classification of Denisovans into three separate populations. A geneticist by the name of Guy Jacobs identified and outlined these populations in 2019, separating them by region into Siberia, East Asia, and New Guinea, including some surrounding islands. Oceania and a few more locales across Asia are also included among the locations that Denisovans had reached.

The Denisovan population whose remains were found in the Denisova Cave most likely branched off as a distinct group some 283,000 years ago and once before, around 363,000 years ago. Contemporary DNA analyses suggest that Denisovans quite likely crossed the Wallace Line at some point, moving into Wallacea and Sahul, which are biogeographical designations for New Guinea and Australia, respectively. A 19th-century British naturalist devised the Wallace line by the name of Alfred Russel Wallace to separate the fauna of Australia and Asia in the interest of classification.

What's unclear is how much water, if any, Denisovans had to cross in order to arrive at those northwestern reaches of Australia. Sea levels were lower during this time, so there were land bridges where none exist today, but it's still very likely that some bodies of water had to be conquered. How Denisovans could have accomplished this feat is one of the many mysteries surrounding them.

According to some estimates regarding the genetic introgression from Denisovans to anatomically modern humans, it's possible that some fragments of Denisovan populations might have survived until as recently as 14,500 years ago. These latest confirmed introgressions occurred primarily in and around New Guinea, suggesting that a Denisovan population might have survived around these parts quite sometime after they had died out elsewhere, including Siberia.

It appears that Denisovans in the Altai Mountains around the Denisova Cave were fairly isolated from other Denisovan populations. However, within this population, they were fairly genetically homogeneous, much more so than contemporary human populations, for instance. We don't know yet how genetically diverse other Denisovan populations were, but it's possible that there was much more diversity than in the region around the Denisova Cave.

The historical range that Denisovans had inhabited shows us a plethora of very different environments, which was sure to impact the populations living there and, over time, lead to distinct adaptations. The environments around the two cave sites, for instance, are and always have been very different. Altitude, humidity, flora, and terrain configuration are all very different. On top of that, Denisovans who reached Southeast Asia had likely "settled" in jungle regions, which is yet another strikingly different environment. The fact that Denisovans had managed to reach and then survive in such dramatically different environments testifies that they were indeed very adaptable, although probably not on the level of Homo sapiens, who has proven to be the undisputed master of adaptation.

The Appearance Discussion

Two primary schools of thought can perhaps be distinguished when it comes to understanding what Denisovans might have looked like. The first school, focusing on a combination of anatomical indicators and genetic studies, believes that we can conclude some things about what Denisovans looked like and that we already have some concrete ideas. On the other hand, there are those that question such theories and believe that we more-or-less have no idea what Denisovans looked like.

The Denisovan finger bone fragment that was discovered is actually not that different from what we would expect from the average Homo sapiens female today. It's the teeth that have given researchers mixed signals, though. Some molars point to robust sets of teeth reminiscent of some of our distant ancestors, as we mentioned earlier, but not all of them are the same. All the discovered molars are outside the range of modern humans, but there are significant variations when they are compared against the teeth of long-gone ancestors like *Homo habilis, Homo rudolfensis, Homo erectus*, and others.

Closer studies of the *Xiahe* mandible have shown some similarities with Neanderthals. For instance, both Denisovans and Neanderthals seem to have had gaps behind their molars while their frontal teeth were flattened. The Denisovan lower jaw's mandibular body was not as high as that of Neanderthals, though, and there were additional differences in the body of the jawbone. Some structural bone similarities exist between Denisovans and *H. erectus*, such as that of the parietal skull bone.

One of the more controversial breakthroughs has been the effort to conduct facial reconstruction and get an idea of what live Denisovans looked like. Unfortunately, everything that researchers have been able to generate has been based almost exclusively on genetics, which leaves a lot of room for skepticism without quality bone specimens to back the claims up. The reconstructions have pointed out numerous facial similarities with Neanderthals, including large noses, sloped foreheads, longer and flattened skulls, long and broad faces, protruding jaws, et cetera. Studies into the possible skeletal structure of Denisovans suggest that they had wide chests and hips as well. A lot of the work on Denisovan facial reconstruction has been carried out in Israel by Liran Carmel of the Hebrew University of Jerusalem and his colleagues.

John Hawks of the University of Wisconsin-Madison has been one of the leading skeptics when it comes to these methods. He believes that

DNA sequences can't tell us much about bone morphology, meaning that any DNA-based facial reconstructions are questionable at best. One of the issues with this approach is that it primarily tells us the ways in which Denisovans looked different from us, which might not necessarily give us an accurate idea of what they actually looked like. We can determine if their foreheads were broader, for example, but it's difficult to ascertain by how much. Sheela Athreya of Texas A&M University was also skeptical, pointing out that such reconstruction efforts ultimately rely on too many assumptions. As of right now, this is, unfortunately, the best method we have, and it gives us at least a partial picture and something to go on, even though it should always come with a grain of salt until more physical evidence is discovered.

The Future of Denisovan Study

The true value of the Denisovan discovery is in its contribution to burying an outdated worldview and idea about how we have evolved. This idea has long reigned supreme in paleoanthropology, believing that human evolution was linear. This simplistic view postulates that it was a simple and straightforward process of one species evolving into the next and continuing step-by-step until we eventually emerged. Numerous paleoanthropologists have challenged such a view for decades, but discoveries such as those surrounding Denisovans have strengthened these ideas.

Instead of being a straight, step-by-step line, experts suggest, human evolution was probably more like a river delta. Our genus Homo has had many individual streams that form that delta, branching out on all sides, going in and out, and occasionally connecting with each other, some leading into new streams and others going off into nothing. What all of this means is that the evolutionary history of our genus is much more complex and chaotic than we thought, even though the process is undoubtedly completely subordinate to the laws of evolution. These various branches met each other at different times and places, and all sorts of mixing occurred left and right. Archaic peoples met each other, genes were exchanged, and natural selection, both positive and negative, took care of the rest.

Given the scarcity of material evidence that we have, it's rather impressive just how much information we have been able to extract about Denisovans. The truth is that Denisovan studies have also been helped by a fair amount of good old luck. Paleoanthropology has found many much younger fossils yet far worse preserved than those in the Denisova Cave. It just isn't every day that fossils will provide such quality DNA samples that can allow geneticists to sequence entire genomes. Other sites have given many bones yet far fewer stories, whereas the Denisova Cave has allowed us to create an entire species' outline based on little more than bits and fragments.

The list of specimens confirmed to have come from Denisovans comes to a grand total of seven, six of which came from the Denisova Cave, while only one originates from Baishiya. The specimen named Denisova 3, also known as X Woman, is a tiny finger bone fragment. Denisova 4 and 8 are permanent upper molars that belonged to adult males living quite a long time apart. Denisova 2 is a lower molar, although deciduous, having belonged to an adolescent female, while Denisova 13 is a skull bone fragment that was only discovered in 2019 and is still undergoing examination. Of course, the last two specimens are the Xiahe mandible and Denisova 11, also known as Denny, who left behind a bone fragment that was part of either an arm or leg.

As you can see, it doesn't take a lot of blind optimism to see that the study of Denisovans has a very bright future. The Denisova Cave may yield further discoveries, which are bound to tell us much more about these archaic hominins, taking the site's track record thus far. Even the specimens that we have already discovered have the potential to give us new information as studies continue and methods improve. In the end, though, it all comes down to luck, and researchers can do little more than keep excavating and surveying while hoping the future will be kind enough to unlock more of the secrets of our past for us.

Chapter Seven:

The Genetic Legacy of Our Cousins

T hroughout this book, there have been mentions of interbreeding between different species or subspecies of archaic humans among themselves but also with us, *Homo sapiens.* We have only sporadically touched upon the implications of this mixing and how it has affected us, but in this chapter, we will take a much closer look at what paleoanthropologists know about this interbreeding and how it has altered our evolutionary path.

The study of Denisovans and other archaic humans is, after all, motivated primarily by our desire to learn more about ourselves and where we come from. Of course, there's also always the plain old thirst for knowledge and scientific discovery, but most of us simply can't help but view everything we learn through the lenses of our own destiny. As such, every contact our species has made with any other group is important, and every insight infinitely valuable.

A History of Intermingling

The evidence that we have tells us that interbreeding between modern and archaic humans occurred mostly during the Middle Paleolithic or the period between 300,000 and 30,000 years ago, as well as the early Upper Paleolithic (Late Stone Age), which corresponds roughly to the period between 50,000 and 12,000 years ago. As mentioned earlier, we now know that these encounters, at different locations and points in time, involved Neanderthals, Denisovans, *H. sapiens*, but most likely also other hominins that are yet to be identified.

Estimates vary, but paleoanthropologists and geneticists generally believe that the transference of Neanderthal genes to early modern humans occurred between 47,000 and 65,000 years ago. As for Denisovans, they most likely left their genetic imprint on us at some point between 44,000 and 54,000 years ago. Between these two archaic human species, there is no doubt that Neanderthals have genetically affected us way more than Denisovans.

Traces of Neanderthal DNA can be found in contemporary human populations in almost all corners of the world, although to varying degrees. For instance, East Asians generally have the highest Neanderthal presence in their genomes, while Southeast Asians have much less and Europeans are somewhere in between. Overall, human populations beyond Sub-Saharan Africa have 1-4% Neanderthal DNA in their genomes. Neanderthal DNA is certainly not unheard of in Africa, but the incidence is much lower. Research has also shown a considerable presence of Neanderthal DNA among Native Americans and Australo-Melanesians, even higher than among Europeans.

Denisovan admixture is much rarer and is generally non-existent among the populations of Africa and western Eurasia. The greatest prevalence of these genes is found across Oceania and parts of Southeast Asia. As you can guess, based on the aforementioned historical range of Denisovans, Melanesians are among the folks who have the greatest Denisovan admixture. Overall, some 4-6% of the contemporary Melanesian genome comes from Denisovans, which is a very significant admixture. Traces of Denisovan DNA occur sporadically elsewhere in Asia, such as in South Asia.

Africa stands out as the location where archaic human genes have been detected in today's populations without being actually identified. Indeed, several distinct sources of genetic admixture have been found, but researchers are still to determine which archaic humans these genes had originated from.

Human evolution was seen as a much more linear and simplistic process in the earlier days of paleoanthropology than it actually was. More recent revelations and all the information we have access to today have told us a story of consistent mixing and hybridization throughout modern humans' evolutionary path. Hybridization was once believed to have been a very rare occurrence and an exception, but more and more scientists are now suggesting that it was actually the rule and that it played one of the decisive roles in the process that made us who we are today.

Hans Peder Steensby first brought up the idea that modern humans might have interbred with Neanderthals in 1907. In fact, he advocated a theory that all humans came from very mixed ancestry. These views were met with controversy at that time because Neanderthals were believed to be much more primitive and ape-like than we now know. Impressively enough, Steensby devised his interbreeding proposition based on physical appearance, including cranial characteristics.

Steensby simply identified such physical similarities between Neanderthals and certain European peoples and concluded that mixing had occurred in prehistoric times. However, Steensby and other paleoanthropologists at the time believed that Neanderthals were direct ancestors to humans, which we now know is not the case. Steensby's proposals remained controversial for decades after he had made them public, and many if not most experts in the field were very slow to accept that our species shared such affinity with Neanderthals.

The Results

The genetic legacy that modern humans carry from Neanderthals, Denisovans, and other archaic humans has had very real effects. We have acquired numerous adaptations and outright benefits from these genes, which have made us stronger in a number of important ways. Of course, these adaptations are more prevalent in some populations than in others, depending on where in the world early modern humans mingled the most with other archaic humans.

When it comes to Neanderthal influence, their genes have led to all sorts of physical alterations in *Homo sapiens* populations that they encountered. These changes and adaptations have affected our sugar metabolism, muscle contractions, keratin filaments, brain size, brain functionality, distribution of body fat, the thickness of enamel, et cetera. Neanderthal admixture has also affected human genes related to things like hair morphology and skin pigmentation. In some populations, there are even indications that Neanderthal admixture affected their immune systems.

Among Europeans and East Asians, the genes that have affected keratin, the main substance that produces things like hair and nails, have played an important role. These genes have affected the hair and skin of the aforementioned populations by giving them certain morphological adaptations that have proven useful in environments beyond Africa. Just as useful were the Neanderthal contributions to the immune systems of modern humans. Interbreeding contributed valuable adaptations that made these humans migrating out of Africa better suited to fend off local pathogens as they moved into Eurasia. These adaptations came in the form of new HLA (human leukocyte antigen) alleles, which are proteins that play a central role in regulating the immune system.

The gene that regulates brain volume, known as microcephalin, has been affected by Neanderthal admixture starting some 37,000 years ago. As usual with Neanderthals, this genetic material is found primarily among Eurasian populations. This particular genetic contribution, generally referred to as haplogroup D, is certain to have come from an archaic human species, but some experts have challenged the theory of Neanderthal origin. Even though there are indications that it indeed wasn't the Neanderthals, no viable alternative source has yet been identified.

Interbreeding with Denisovans often had similar positive results on human evolutionary progress by making them a better-adapted, more versatile species that could adapt to most corners of the world. However, when it comes to Denisovans, we know less than we do about our intermingling with Neanderthals simply because we have less evidence. As you know, Denisovans are a recent discovery, so we may learn about other ways they affect our genome in the future. There is, however, one reason why their genetic contribution has been smaller is the somewhat frequent infertility of male hybrids.

Be that as it may, there are solid indications that Denisovans, too, have affected the immune systems of the modern humans that they encountered. One of the HLA alleles found in modern human immune systems, referred to as HLA-B*73, has likely originated from Denisovans. Studies into this possibility have focused especially on western Asia. Other HLA alleles might have been introduced into the gene pool by Denisovans. As with Neanderthals, early modern humans probably picked these genes up as they moved into the Denisovan habitat, helping them adapt more easily and boost their defenses against new diseases.

We also briefly mentioned earlier how Denisovan DNA most likely affected certain Tibetan populations. The advantageous gene variants that these folks received are EGLN1 and EPAS1. These genes determine people's resistance to hypoxia, and they affect their hemoglobin concentration. The way in which EPAS1 allows humans to cope with low oxygen levels at great altitudes is by increasing their hemoglobin levels, which usually has the drawback of increasing blood viscosity. The EPAS1 variant affected by Denisovan genes, on the other hand, optimizes that hemoglobin increase and provides for more optimal performance at high altitudes.

Red Deer Cave People

When the focus is shifted back to Denisovans, particularly in regard to their interbreeding with modern humans, one discovery that stands out is a certain archaic human population known as the Red Deer Cave people. The remains of these ancient humans were first discovered in Red Deer and Longlin caves, which are located in the Yunnan province of Southwest China. The fossils have been estimated as between 14,500 and 11,500 years old.

Some paleoanthropologists have suggested this to be a new human species or sub-species, but there are strong indications that these are the remains of a hybrid population that emerged from the mingling of Denisovans and *Homo sapiens*. One reason why some paleoanthropologists believe these to be hybrids is that they exhibit a relatively unique mix of modern and archaic human features. Others have challenged this, postulating that the Red Deer Cave people might have just been early modern humans who were simply a bit more robust than usual.

The first fossil discoveries, notably a partial skull, occurred in 1979 in the Longlin Cave, while the first Red Deer Cave specimens were unearthed ten years later. More thorough research, including dating, began only in 2012. The discovery in 1989 was that of a partial thighbone, partial jaw, teeth, and bits of skull. Disagreements began when it came time to date these samples. Anatomically speaking, these fossils generally resembled archaic human ancestors such as the *Homo erectus* or *Homo habilis*, but, as you know, they lived more than a million years ago in Africa. Further study showed it to be highly unlikely that these specimens are anywhere near that old and that they are relatively recent.

Those archaic features that have puzzled paleoanthropologists include flat faces, broad noses, protruding brows, large molar teeth, thick skulls, and somewhat smaller brains. These were smaller hominins that averaged a weight of roughly 110 lb or 50 kg, like many other human ancestors. The uncovered thighbone sample suggests peculiar things about the RDC people's legs, which may have had knock-knees. One of the prominent researchers who studied these remains, Darren Curnoe, has pointed out that these folks had teeth that were strangely similar to archaic humans, considering how relatively recent the fossils are. Curnoe strongly believes that the RDC people represent a distinct human evolutionary line.

Still, most paleoanthropologists are yet to recognize these ancient folks as a new human species. The Denisovan-Modern human hybrid theory is just one explanation that paleoanthropologists have been floating. Some experts have suggested that they might have been fully modern humans who were physiologically different for reasons that are yet to be determined. Unfortunately, researchers have been unable to extract any meaningful DNA samples from the fossils, despite the fact that some of them might have originated as recently as 11,000 years ago.

Another possible explanation is that these folks were the descendants of early humans who migrated from Africa and became isolated before mingling with other species. As such, they might have settled in their locale more than 100,000 years ago. The configuration of the surrounding terrain certainly allows it, thanks to the many mountains and valleys. The climate in southwestern China is unique as well, so, coupled with genetic isolation, it is indeed possible that a group of humans could have evolved in a very distinct manner. Whether new evidence, DNA or otherwise, will emerge remains to be seen. For now, though, the theory of Denisovan hybridization is the most popular one.

Conclusion

Since recorded history and organized civilization account for such a tiny fraction of true human history, we are prone to having our perspective somewhat warped. We have so much information about this one small snippet of human existence and so little about the rest that it's easy to get caught up in recorded history and forget how long the actual human journey has been. Hundreds of thousands of years, and the millions before them, have all played their part in bringing us exactly where we are today.

Thanks to what we now know about our long-gone cousins, such as Neanderthals and Denisovans, we have managed to put quite a few things in perspective. We can now realize that the chapter of history we live in and are influenced by is but a single episode in one long show that our incredible species has witnessed. Since we're the only remaining human species, we can also contemplate how differently history might have gone had things taken just one or two different turns.

These folks of a long-lost era have touched us, though, and parts of them now live within us. They didn't get to see the fruits that would eventually sprout from human civilization, but the genetic contributions they have given us have made us what we are today. 50,000 or more years ago, people probably didn't concern themselves with much more than staying alive and having their next meal. Still, unknowingly, each of them participated in one grand process that has led to the developments we now take for granted. Among these developments is our ability to peek into our past like never before and truly appreciate just how far we have come.

References

Callaway, E. (2019). First portrait of mysterious Denisovans drawn from DNA. Nature, 573(7775), 475–476. https://doi.org/10.1038/d41586-019-02820-0

Denisova Cave | Facts, Location, & Artifacts. (n.d.). Encyclopedia Britannica. https://www.britannica.com/place/Denisova-Cave

Godfraind, T., & Vercauteren Drubbel, R. (2019). A Brief Account of Human Evolution for Young Minds. Frontiers for Young Minds, 7. https://doi.org/10.3389/frym.2019.00022

Groeneveld, E. (2016, October 21). Neanderthal. Ancient History Encyclopedia. https://www.ancient.eu/Neanderthal/

Groeneveld, E. (2019, March 5). Denisovan. Ancient History Encyclopedia; Ancient History

Encyclopedia. https://www.ancient.eu/Denisovan/

History.com Editors. (2018, August 21). Denisovans. HISTORY. https://www.history.com/topics/pre-history/denisovans

McKie, R. (2018, November 24). Meet Denny, the ancient mixed-heritage mystery girl. The Guardian. https://www.theguardian.com/science/2018/nov/24/denisovan-neanderthal-hybrid-denny-dna-finder-project

Page, M. L. (n.d.). This is almost certainly not what Denisovans looked like. New Scientist. Retrieved from https://www.newscientist.com/article/2216875-this-is-almost-certainly-not-what-denisovans-looked-like/

Warren, M. (2018). Mum's a Neanderthal; Dad's a Denisovan: First discovery of an ancient-human hybrid. Nature, 560(7719), 417–418. https://doi.org/10.1038/d41586-018-06004-0

Wei-Haas, M. (2019a, April 11). Multiple lines of mysterious ancient humans interbred with us. Science. https://www.nationalgeographic.com/science/article/

enigmatic-human-relative-outlived-neander-thals

Wei-Haas, M. (2019b, September 19). DNA reveals first look at enigmatic human relative. Science. https://www.nationalgeographic.com/science/article/dna-reveals-first-look-enigmatic-human-relative

CPSIA information can be obtained
at www.ICGtesting.com
Printed in the USA
LVHW050407291121
704719LV00013B/533